The Perfect Guide to Start Food Truck Business

Recipes idea for food truck

Perry Anderson

Table of Contents

START YOUR OWN FOOD TRUCK BUSINESS TODAY 4

    THE CASE WITH STARTING A GOOD TRUCK BUSINESS 5
    WHY PEOPLE MAY START A FOOD TRUCK BUSINESS 7

STARTING UP YOUR OWN FOOD TRUCK – THE BASICS............10

QUESTIONS TO ASK YOURSELF BEFORE OPENING A FOOD TRUCK ...12

THE MOST INTEGRAL FACTORS OF STARTING A FOOD TRUCK BUSINESS 14

    LEGALITIES 14
    VEHICLES 15
    BRAND 15
    FINANCING 16

DO YOU HAVE OPTIONS? YES, YOU DO... FOR YOUR FOOD TRUCK BUSINESS 18

THE HOW'S OF RUNNING A FOOD TRUCK BUSINESS.......................19

    WHAT ABOUT THAT LOCATION? 20

ALL ABOUT THE COSTS... OF STARTING A FOOD TRUCK 22

    SELECTING THE RIGHT FOOD TRUCK? NOT ALL FOOD TRUCKS ARE THE SAME.... 25
    GETTING LICENSES AND PERMITS FOR YOUR FOOD TRUCK 27

MAKE THE BEST POSSIBLE PRODUCT: 32

FOOD PLANS FOR FOOD TRUCKS 32

    CONSIDERATIONS FOR YOUR MENU... TO GET THAT MENU RIGHT 32
    BUILDING YOUR FOUNDATION OF RECIPES 35

YOUR FOOD TRUCK, THE MENU AND THE RECIPES 38

GETTING STARTED... WITH RECIPE 39

DEVELOPMENT FOR FOOD TRUCKS 39
    The Menu and Recipes 40
THE COST OF FOOD FOR FOOD TRUCK 42
BUSINESSES...42
    Behind Food Truck Menu Costs..43
WHAT TO CONSIDER ABOUT PORTION CONTROL 48
    Let's Make a Well Balanced Food Truck Menu 50
RECIPES, FOOD TRUCK MENUS... AND PREPARING THEM ALL..........53
    Food Ideas For Food Trucks? 53
    Recipe Ideas For Food Truck Menus.................................54
    Barbeque 55
BBQ TURKEY LEGS 56
THAI BBQ GRILLED CHICKEN RECIPE 58
CUPCAKES AND OTHER SWEET TREATS..61
    Vanilla and Chocolate Chip Cupcakes..............................62
DIFFERENT TYPES OF SANDWICHES 65
SIMPLE CHICKEN PANINI 67
TRY YOUR REGIONAL CUISINE 69
SWEET POTATO STEAK FRIES 71
CLASSIC STEAK FAJITAS 73
DON'T FORGET ABOUT LOCAL ORGANIC FARE, TOO 76
COZY VEGETARIAN CHILI 78
ARE YOU READY TO GET INTO THE MOBILE FOOD BUSINESS? 81
CONCLUSION..83

3

Start Your Own Food Truck Business Today

Believe it or not, one of the 'hottest' commodities in the business start-up world is the food truck business. Nowadays, more and more people are finding reasons to start their own food truck business—and, it's not just because of the food, either.

According to research firms that have explored the mobile food industry, mobile food trucks and other non-mechanized carts actually became a 'billion dollar industry with an impressive growth rate of 8.4 percent since the years 2007 to 2012.' Just by looking that those figures, the mobile food industry looks like a good one to break out a business in, right? That's not all.

The Case with Starting a Good Truck Business

Starting a food truck business pretty much places people right in the middle of a wide base of consumers. In other words, anyone who is, well, hungry can benefit from using a food truck, especially since many popular food trucks often cater to several groups of people at once.

Many popular food trucks also extensively travel, reaching many different demographics of potential customers across their city and even multiple cities at a time. You'll usually see some kind of food truck in your city's downtown area, though they usually also reside at places like transport (bus and train) stations, conference centers, resorts, airports and stadiums.

Since food trucks are mobile in nature, they can be literally taken anywhere the owner thinks they can get business. And, most of the time, they do end up getting plenty of business. Though, why are food trucks as popular as a potential business option, anyway?

Many experts in the food industry assume that the mobile food business has seen a large boost in business over the past few years, due to the economy's slow growth over the past few years. Instead of spending more on breakfast and lunch, many people instead seek meals from food trucks.

Food trucks also provide a better alternative meal for people who are now pressed for time during the day. Since a lot of people may have longer work hours and/or shorter lunch hours, getting meals from a food truck is typically a better alternative than having to make and take their own meals from home.

So, due to those particular factors, the mobile food industry is more or less a good industry for people to try their hand in. In fact, if you have a passion for running what's essentially your own mobile restaurant, why not try building your own food truck business?

Why People May Start a Food Truck Business

There are many reasons why people choose to start their own business—and it's usually due to personal reasons that ultimately benefit them in the long run. If you're looking for a stable business, you might get into the mobile food industry to manage your own seasonal food truck. Others may want to start a specialty food cart simply because they know it will make them money... because they have the drive and passion for food to make it a successful endeavor.

Though, you also have to remember the benefits to starting a food truck, too. Food trucks not only provide budding and seasoned entrepreneurs with benefits, but the customers see benefits, too. Let's take a look at some of the benefits that a food truck can provide, as paraphrased from a source about the food truck industry:

Entrepreneurs can benefit from the low overhead costs that are associated with starting a food truck business. The vehicles that are used to house all of the necessary components for the food truck – carts, trailers, kiosks and food trucks themselves – don't absorb many costs like a stationary building would. Instead, these vehicles allow an entrepreneur to save on having to rent an entire building to house their restaurant business. Since they're mobile, all they need to do is move the entire truck to another location if they don't see business in certain areas.

Customers can benefit from food trucks due to the sheer convenience of having one around. And, as many people would attest to food trucks, having one around when you need it is a good thing. A very good thing. Many people actually like the inconvenience due to the fact that they usually don't have to wait long to get any food and drink—they can just head to the nearest food cart and immediately get what they need.

We do suggest running a food truck business for a variety of reasons, though the main reason pretty much involves having a consistent source of income—and, that's not even taking the relative job security this particular job provides, either. As long as you approach this business opportunity with determination and an open mind, you can succeed having your own mobile truck business.

Though, you're probably wondering how you can start your own mobile truck business. Well, you're in luck. In this book, we're going to talk about the many things that go into running a mobile truck business, in addition to what you foods you can plan to sell—with a side of recipes, too!

Starting Up Your Own Food Truck – The Basics

The food truck industry is one of the fastest growing industries for a reason. The business is pretty simple for entrepreneurs to grasp, while customers can't seem to get enough of food trucks in their cities. So, now that you see how popular food trucks can be, how can any well-meaning person get started with their own food truck business?

To start, even though starting a food truck is considered easier than starting a restaurant, it's still difficult to get off the ground if you're not prepared to put in the effort to make it work. Food trucks can become incredibly prone to succumbing to the elements and be subject to many other harmful outside factors like other vehicles, theft, vandalism and even unexpected fire hazards.

Sometimes, working a food truck during certain seasons is grounds for not getting any sales. I mean, you don't want to run your food truck in the winter... when you're selling mostly frozen treats like ice cream. The hours can be long, too—some food trucks stay out from 9 in the morning to as last as 5 in the afternoon on a regular schedule, while others end up spending the entire day and night in a single spot.

Despite those very real concerns, starting a food truck is still a great way to get started as an entrepreneur in general. And, if you're especially passionate about food, perhaps starting a food truck is very much for you.

Questions to Ask Yourself Before Opening a Food Truck

Starting any business takes time. Though, as long as you take the time to start a business, you don't have to worry about any potential faults that may arise when running the business itself. That notion also applies to people who expect to get into the mobile food industry, though don't expect to get involved in the industry... until they're about to contribute.

Though, before you figure out what type of food truck you're planning to open, it's important to ask yourself questions about what you may expect out of the business. Those questions may include:

- What's my passion in food?
- What type of food do I want to serve?
- What type of food may be missing from my community?
- Are there other food trucks with the same concepts/food products as mine?

- How can I differentiate my brand from other brands?
- How much money will I have to initially invest in this business?
- Where am I going to get the food that I'm planning to serve in my business?
- How much do I need to invest in those products?

Asking questions simply helps remove the uncertainty associated with starting a food truck business. In fact, for a lot of people, knowing more about what to expect from a food truck business makes them more comfortable with starting the business in the first place, since they do know what to expect after doing the research.

After you learn more about what to expect, there are other factors that you have to take into consideration, particularly when you're, you guessed it, considering starting a food truck business. A lot of those factors are a pretty integral part of the business itself, making it pretty important to pay attention to them.

The Most Integral Factors of Starting a Food Truck Business

The most integral factors of starting a food truck business are pretty straightforward when you think about it. They're very much the same factors involved with starting other businesses since; you pretty much need to take care of those things before setting out on the road for the first time!

The depth that these factors take on is something that we're going to cover in the following sections, if you wanted to know. Though, before then, let's take a look at these factors, as paraphrased from a mobile food industry resource:

Legalities

Understandingly, you can't exactly run a food truck business without seeking some type of permit from your city and country jurisdiction. Having a permit that's specifically designed to cover a mobile business takes care of, well, the legalities associated with running such a business and operating the vehicle within your city.

At best, a permit adequately covers running most aspects of your mobile food truck, unless you need additional legal permissions from your city or county jurisdiction.

Vehicles

Naturally, you have to find a truck to conduct and transport your business anywhere you need it to travel. Now, you don't exactly have to spend a lot of money on a food truck. Many food-ready trucks and/or trailers can cost as low as $1,500 USD and as high as $75,000, depending on the type of truck you might plan to eventually buy.

Ultimately, you want to go for a truck or food-ready vehicle that's big enough to house the business and last a while.

Brand

If you want your food truck to catch on, you'll have to establish a brand. A brand is what helps potential customers immediately recognize a business, especially if that business is already pretty popular. As a food truck owner, you're going to want people to remember the name of your business and the foods you eat, so start brainstorming names and ideas that might foster what you envision your business being.

Names are also just one part of establishing a business; you also have to come up with a potential menu, figure out what supplies and foods to buy and organize anything you want to address before even getting the legal paperwork out of the way.

Financing

Arguably the most important aspect of starting a food truck. Why? It's mainly because you literally can't do much with little to no financing. You can't even buy the truck! So, before you get into the entire planning aspect, look for potential private vendors.

You'll have the best luck searching for a private investor who may be interested in backing your food truck business, though that rarely happens unless an investor really happens to like your vision and your food. You can always head to your bank to get a loan, especially if you qualify for any of their financing options—naturally, you can always seek help from an alternative financial institution if you don't want to use a bank.

Financing a food truck usually includes covering costs for the truck, branding, equipment, food and its associated supplies, point-of-sale (POS) or credit card systems, safety precautions and, sometimes, employees.

So, as you can see, there are several factors that go into starting your own food truck business. While we just covered those particular factors in brief here, we'll review these concepts and expand on them a little more lately. Though, for now, let's take a look at your options when it comes to starting your very own food truck business.

Do You Have Options? Yes, You Do... For Your Food Truck Business

You have options. But, where do you have options? Well, you have options when starting your own food truck business, of course!

So, where do you start? One of the first things you have to consider when you're about to start a food truck business is, well, the foods you're planning to sell. Though, before you think about *what* type of food you may sell in your food truck, it's important to wonder about the *hows* of running a food truck business.

The How's of running a Food Truck Business

It's always important to know 'how' you're going to handle something. That especially goes for if you're planning on starting a business—any type of business, in fact. When it comes to running a food truck business, a lot of those *hows* merely consist of considerations you should make for the sake of properly running your food truck business.

So, what do you need to think about before you start shopping around for the right food truck? Well, you need to know:

❖ How much funds will you have at start-up, in addition to the total budget of your business and the possible potential of returns on investment.
❖ How committed you expect to remain to your business, whether you plan on working part-time, full time or a combination of shifts.

- How creative your ideas may be, and whether you will push your limits to fulfill them.
- How experienced you are with running a business of that caliber.
- How big you actually want your food truck business to be at the start.
- How you can eventually reach your 'target demographic' to eventually maximize your sales.

Of course, there's always room for more questions. Though, those '*hows*' are probably the most important *hows* you should think about before thinking about the '*what's*'... and maybe, the *what-now's*.

What about That Location?

The location where you start your food truck business can actually 'make or break' your success. Don't know how that works? It's simple: some locations simply take to food trucks more than others. And, that usually has a lot to do with parking laws, the people that live there and the potential competition that resides there, too.

Of course, many major cities like New York and San Francisco are packed with incredible food trucks—and they're all vying for everyone's attention. Even in smaller cities, it can be difficult to find a prime spot to attract people who may want to do business. Couple that with parking laws and you might have more trouble finding a spot than you thought.

Though, if you're a little creative, you can find a choice location to park your business to, well, do business. Always check with your local area's parking laws before finding the right spot to situate your business. And, of course, don't forget to think about the costs, too.

All about the Costs... of Starting a Food Truck

Don't think that you just need to spend a few thousand on a food truck business—it's not that frugal of a business. There are many factors you have to think about before getting to a point where you can comfortably be sure about the amount of money you're putting into that same business. Because, it will take quite a few funds to ensure that your food truck gets off to a great start.

So, what costs actually go into a food truck business? Well, that's simple to answer. One of the more interesting things to note about a food truck business is that much of the costs will be partially reserved for legal fees, specifically those associated with getting appropriate permits, insurance and legal aid.//
And, some of those legalities are actually 'time-gated' in some states, or, in other words, require some time on a wait-list before receiving one. Can you guess what that particular legality involves? That's right—

getting the Mobile Food Vending Unit Permit to actually operate your truck!

Some of the costs also involve getting potential employees up to speed, too. Many food truck vendors have a hand or two to keep their business running smoothly, so that's something to keep in mind if you're planning on running a relatively large food truck business.

Now, let's take a look at a cost breakdown for the average food truck business. These figures, paraphrased from a food truck resource, actually account for figures derived from the East Coast region of the United States—specifically (and naturally) New York City. So, if you're planning on starting a food truck on the East Coast, these figures are a pretty good estimate to use as a guideline if you're already anticipating the costs.

All figures are estimates, East Coast USA
- ❖ **Truck** – $50,000 (covers the cost of purchase and basic retrofitting)

- **Mobile Food Vending Unit Permit** – $200 + potential wait-listing (may cost $15,000 if acquired through third parties)
- **Commissary** – $500 per month; expected to cost at least $6,000 per year.
- **General Liability Insurance, business** – $3,500 to $4,000 per year
- **Mobile Vendors License** – about $100 (accounts for about $50 for classes and $50 for 2-year license)
- **Truck Insurance** – about $2,000 to $3,000 per year (estimates point to $2,500 per year)
- **Commercial Kitchen** – about $2,000 to $5,000 per month (estimates point to an $36,000 per year)
- **Employee Wages** – about $16 per hour (estimates vary throughout year)
- **Workers Compensation** – about $7,000 per year (accounts for 3 employees, may vary based on number of employees)
- **Accountant** – about $350 per month (accounts for about $4,200 per year)
- **PR Professional** – about $1,500 for about 3 months (accounts for at least $6,000 per year)

When you add up all of those costs, the total cost of running a food truck business rounds out to about $150,000 to $200,000—and, that's just taking the average cost into account. Still, a food truck business can be rewarding, and rewarding enough to make well enough profits to cover those spent costs.

Selecting the Right Food Truck? Not All Food Trucks are the same....

Not all food trucks are made the same, but they all pretty much serve the same purpose. Food trucks, in fact, are known for carrying the equipment needed to prepare, cook, store and serve different types of foods. And, given that those basic functions are what define the 'food truck,' you shouldn't really look for something that's too complicated on your first venture as a food truck vendor.

Most traditional food trucks provide lunches, so they're naturally equipped with all the tools to prepare various lunch-worthy foods. Foods like stocking sandwiches, tacos, burgers and kebobs are some of the food truck staples that regularly find themselves on the menus of many food trucks. Besides those staples, many food truck vendors now carry many vegetarian and vegan options to provide a truly diverse food selection.

You're going to want a good food truck for two main reasons. The first reason involves the fact that food trucks are large enough to handle anything you throw at them—in terms of preparing and storing food on board. It just eliminates the trouble with dealing a smaller food cart. The second involves the fact that food trucks are a lot simpler to manage on a daily basis.

There are actually two types of food trucks you should watch out for on the market:

Mobile food preparation vehicle (MFPV). This truck allows you to prepare food on the truck after customers make their order. Most customers do have to wait a while to get their order, though this truck type essentially allows you to prepare fresh meals on board.

Industrial catering vehicle (ICV). This vehicle is pretty straightforward in function. It's the type of food truck that simply sells prepackaged foods—and nothing else. This is probably the first food truck you'll have, if you're passionate about the business.

Mobile food preparation vehicles naturally cost more than an industrial catering vehicle, thanks to the nature of their functions. To give you an idea, many MPFV food trucks are known to cost upwards of $30,000, depending on condition. Industrial catering vehicles cost thousands of dollars less. New and/or custom MFPV vehicles are known to cost as much as $100,000.

You don't have to settle for a $100,000 food truck, though. There are many lower priced options that can do just what you need it to do. Long before you finalize your purchase of a food truck, you need to make sure all of your legalities are taken care of. What legalities, you mean? The legalities involved with getting the appropriate licenses and permits.

Getting Licenses and Permits for Your Food Truck

Getting the licenses and permits for your food truck is probably the most important part of the preparation process—the process of preparing to open your own food truck business. A lot of people don't consider this part of the process exciting, but it's a necessary part for people that believe in starting their business in the only way possible.

One of the biggest focuses with getting a permit and license is adhering to the official codes and regulations associated with starting a food truck business. Food trucks, in fact, used to have a questionable stigma, until stricter health codes and sanitary regulations were introduced across the United States.

To get started, you can always contact your state's local department of health to learn more information about handling a food-related business. On an interesting note, the types of foods you handle may change the definition of what you're supposed to represent in accordance with current health regulations. People that sell prepackaged foods aren't considered food handlers, and typically have less requirements appointed to them than a person that handles food.

People that deal with unwrapped food and take care of their preparation are known as food handlers, so they naturally have specific regulations they must meet before they start handling food on a daily basis, all to meet their state's health standards.

Of course, anyone who wants to run a good truck should know that they're subject to getting evaluated by a health inspector on occasions, notably when you first establish your business. To provide an example, a health inspector may request information to verify factors as seen in the following paraphrased list from another East Coast location within the United States:

- A proof of ownership, proper license and/or identification for the vehicle.
- A District Food Manager Identification Card
- A food-purchase record storage and/or record keeping.

- Proof that your commissary, service support facility and/or depot meet the vending unit's operation needs.
- A copy of your service support facility's license and/or a recently conducted inspection's report.

Most food trucks and other food-related vehicles are inspected at least once every year. Many of these inspections happen on a random basis, so, as a food truck vendor, you should be prepared for when the occasion happens.

Health inspectors generally check your food storage methods, mainly seeing if your storage methods spoil food and if that food's being stored at the correct temperature. They also check all of the associated equipment that you may use to prepare various foods, in addition to any sinks and/or water supplies stored in the vehicle.

They also check the garages and/or commercial kitchen associated with a food truck, typically on a frequent basis. This ensures that those facilities are kept up to current health standards, especially if associated with a food truck.

Besides the permits and the licenses, you have to think about financing. Though, before we go into depth about financing, let's take a look at the most important component of your food truck business—the food.

Make the Best Possible Product: Food Plans For Food Trucks

Now, for the food. Food is a big part of food trucks – naturally – and that makes choosing the right food for your truck important. Though, while you can pick the foods that you like the most as centerpieces for the main menu, you also have to take 'regional tastes' into consideration, too.

Considerations for Your Menu... To Get That Menu Right

Just look at all of the other food trucks, carts, trailers and kiosks on the market today and see what's on their menu. Lots of stuff, right? Although some of those menus look 'disorganized,' they're actually a good selection of foods and beverages that people just love.

Though, you can't just include all of the foods that people love. Take something as complicated as lasagna.

You may have to pay more to have pasta dishes like that made, frozen and shipped to you—if you're not preparing it yourself. And, you also have to think about how long it'll take to reheat that for customers. When you take the costs and preparation time from producing that product into consideration, having comfort foods like lasagna on your menu doesn't see that practical at all.

To avoid issues with both time and money, it's best to keep things simple when you're starting out—trust me, when people dole out that advice, they mean it! You don't want to get stuck preparing something that takes too much time and, eventually, resources out of your operations... when you could be cooking something that takes less time and money to prepare. With practicality in mind, there are other questions you should ask yourself about preparing your food truck's menu. The following questions listed here are paraphrased from another food truck resource:

❖ What can you cook? What foods do you actually like cooking?

- Do you have any popular town, county, city or regional foods?
- What ingredients can you easily buy (in bulk) from markets, farms and/or wholesalers in your area?
- What foods can you easily transport to and from another on-site commercial kitchen?
- What can you prepare and/or heat with no difficulties?
- What foods are best suited for your cooking expertise? What foods will allow you to be creative?
- What foods are easy for customers to carry around?
- What foods will cost the least to produce and sell?
- What foods aren't being sold at other food trucks, carts and other vehicles?
- What time of day will you open for business?
- Are you going to specialize in serving just a few foods? Are you going to have a larger menu?

Once you have a good idea about what you might want to serve, start drafting your menu. That menu could just be notepad scribbles or actual sketches of the dishes you plan to make—it doesn't matter. As long as you write that menu down, it's completely fine! Though, the next step you need to take involves actually formulating your recipes.

Building Your Foundation of Recipes

You need a foundation... a foundation of recipes for your food truck. So, once you've figured out an appropriate menu, take the time to start researching and brainstorming the exact recipes you want to include on your menu.

We say brainstorm and research because you're not only going to be creating your own recipes, but you can also include 'tried and true' recipes to help keep your customers coming back for your own take on classic favorites.

So, how can you get started perfecting those recipes of yours? That's pretty simple. You can actually brainstorm, cook those recipes and taste tests them to see if they're 'good enough' to include on your menu. It doesn't hurt to bring in some friends and family members to test your recipes, too. You can get valuable feedback from them, so you'll know what to change and what to add to certain recipes that need a little more 'cooking' before you use them.

You're not going to use every recipe that you concoct— the main point of creating, taste testing and perfecting recipes is finding one or two recipes that will best suit your food truck. So, it's natural to only want to include the best recipes possible.

So, when you've found those recipes, just make sure you write them down, too! You did write them down, right? Now that you have, you can actually use those recipes to try and find an appropriate structure for your food truck. Like, if you wanted to have your food truck mostly serve up comfort food, you'd spend a while perfecting a set of classic comfort food dishes for that menu.

You're usually not ready to add something to your menu... until you see how it goes with the other recipes. Sometimes, that single recipe might not even work with your menu at all! You'll have to test many recipes to find the right set that will make your food truck the business you want it to be. There's even a set of guidelines you can use to meet that particular standard for yourself, as paraphrased from a food truck resource:

- ❖ Your recipes should be easy to make in large quantities.
- ❖ Your recipes should produce foods or beverages with a consistently good to great taste.
- ❖ Your recipes should produce foods that are easy to serve.
- ❖ Your recipes should produce foods that will travel well, whether based on temperature or its longevity.

As mentioned, it takes time to find that golden set of recipes that will make your main menu stand out against other similar food trucks. Remember that it takes time to develop a menu that just works, so don't get frustrated about it—stay motivated!

Your Food Truck, the Menu and The Recipes

Did you know that it's not hard to develop recipes for a food truck? It's pretty easy—just takes a look at our last section. Though, our last section talked more about the 'vetting criteria' for picking out the perfect menu for a budding food truck. What about the actual creation process for your recipes?

Your recipes will essentially be the main element separating your food truck from the masses. Why? That same menu of yours, with your uniquely crafted recipes, has the potential to turn your modest food truck into a popular brand that keeps your regulars coming back—and recommending others, too.

In the next section, we're going to review the creation process of recipes for food trucks... and take a look at a few recipes, too.

Getting Started... With Recipe Development for Food Trucks

In the last section, we talked about the process of developing a plan for your food truck business. We didn't go into more detail about how to effectively brainstorm the types of foods you might want to introduce to your business.

We stress the importance of brainstorming the types of foods that you may want because, ultimately, these foods will be the foods that will comprise your eventual menu, so you don't want to not know how to make and later add on more appropriate foods for your menu.

So, before we go into detail about that, what's recipe development anyway? Just by examining both words 'recipe' and 'development,' you should know that recipe development means what it describes: the development of recipes. When you develop food recipes, you're essentially creating recipes after brainstorming what makes them work. And, developing a well-rounded menu is something that you should aim for accomplishing when you're about to start your own food truck business.

The Menu and Recipes

Your food truck menu will pretty much describe the bread and butter of your business: the food and beverage items that you sell. That's why it's important to develop a menu that will effectively show what you're capable of producing, so that every time a person chooses to order food or beverages from you, that they're getting exactly what they want every time they visit you.

As we expressed in the last section, it's not that difficult to develop a menu, nor is it that difficult to develop recipes for the food or beverage items you might want on your menu. And, when you think about it, there are a lot of ways that you can go about building a good menu for your truck business, including:

- Simply writing down food and/or drink items that you want to include.
- Writing down food and/or drink items that may work best for your business, especially in regards to the tastes of your potential consumers.
- Writing down foods and/or drinks that simply sell more for a wide variety of factors, including profit.
- Writing down foods and drinks that you can comfortably reproduce on a daily basis without any cost and/or labor problems.

Of course, those aren't the only ways that you can potentially develop a menu that best suits your food truck business, but it doesn't hurt to try them at least once.

Another thing to think about, that we didn't yet talk about in detail, is the prospect of maintaining your food costs. In other words, what about the cost of all of that food? Food isn't free to make, you know.

The Cost of Food for Food Truck Businesses

Anyone who regularly shops for food knows that food can get expensive, if you're not too careful about the prices in the market. When it comes to starting what's essentially a restaurant business, watching those same costs may get more important than you think.

Two of the most important elements that can influence the cost of a food truck menu is:

- **Portion control**, which naturally involves controlling the amount of food included in servings.
- **Monetary costs**, which involve, well, the actual costs of all of the food items involved in creating the menu used for your food truck.

Even if you assume that you have good control over what you might want to include on your food truck menu, think again. You still have to think about the costs of that same menu—and, we're not just talking about the money aspect, either.

Behind Food Truck Menu Costs

You're not going to build a food truck menu on a budget, but you can budget so you can execute that menu as accurately as you can. That generally involves finding out the total costs of all of the food that you plan to use.

Food cost, as paraphrased from a food-related resource, refers to the exact menu price of a certain dish in correlation to the cost food that's used to create that same dish. Again, in other words, that typically refers to the amount of money that you'll have to charge for that same dish, which is derived from its true cost.

So, you'll basically have to decide how much you'd like to profit off these menu items. You can always control the mark-up and have that same mark-up add about 50% of its original price to its menu price. After a certain percentage, a lot of food truck menu items can simply become ridiculously profitable, but you have to take the cost to make them into account.

Remember when we talked a little about food cost in relation to your budget in the last section? Well, we're bringing that up again. Because, your budget usually plays a large role in how you decide to price your menu items.

Now, most food costs are determined by adding mark-up to the costs of your menu items. The 'normal' rates usually add about 30% to about 45% percent to the original cost to make the menu item. Some food truck vendors add a little more of a mark-up to their menu items, simply because of another set of factors involved with the preparation of food truck items. Let's take a look at those factors:

The cost to make. Self explanatory. This figure is usually derived from the actual prices of the ingredients that went into making the food on your menu. So, if you were going to sell pita sandwiches, to provide an example, you'd add up the costs of all of the food you used to make them, and probably divide them by a value, typically the amount of food you're going to make.

Now, it's not just about the cost to make... it's also about the costs associated with:

- Preparing the food and/or hiring someone else to help prepare the food.
- Serving the food, which usually includes wrapping, packing and serving food for customers?
- Cleaning up after the food preparation process, which includes cleaning up the leftover food and supplies from cooking and serving up different menu items?

Of course, all of those 'parameters' vary when you put different food trucks into the equation. Some of the 'fanciest' food trucks have a higher mark-up behind their actual costs, thanks to the fact that it merely takes more work to produce their often high end meals.

Usually adding and/or subtracting elements from your food truck menu items will significantly bring down costs.... or raise them higher. That's because every element that goes into your menu dishes does influence the final costs—to the point of raising the final price of that particular menu item.

So, how do you price those particular menu items? Well, the actual formula that people use to figure out their prices is generally expressed like, according to our paraphrased food truck source:

❖ The cost of your (food product)/0.XX=menu price for your product (written as '$XX.XX/.XX=$XX.XX as an example')

The price that you get is naturally the price that correlates with those prices of your soon-to-be menu items. Sometimes, however, there are some prices that just don't work in the eyes of consumers, such as 'awkward' price points like '$10.78' and vice versa.

Those particular prices can actually be modified to suit the buying tastes of consumers, since they do pay attention to different price points. So, you can get away with bumping up that $10.78 to a more appropriate $10.99 to get rid of that physiological factor that may stop customers from buying menu items that they might have liked... if it weren't for the price!

What to Consider About Portion Control

When you think about it, portion control is far more important than you think. In fact, portion control affects many factors of the entire menu planning process—the costs, the foods and beverages that you might want to carry and the recipes themselves. You're probably wondering how portion control can hold such a large influence over your menu... and that's a good question to have. You see, the portions that you divide your dishes into pretty much help you figure out how much you need to make—every time.

Let's think about our favorite restaurants – and even food trucks – for a moment. Do you know that there's a certain amount of food that has to go into each dish that's made—every time that it's made?

Those amounts of food actually help chefs and their accompanying cooks know how much to put into every dish they make, each time they make those same dishes. Portion control, in that respect, pretty much helps them keep track of the food they may make every day.

Can you imagine making certain dishes, but making too much of one dish? Too little of another dish on your menu? Can you imagine how much it would cost to recoup lost costs from an 'overproduced' dish... if it wasn't popular with your customers? While there are rare dishes that, well, just work with customers, other dishes aren't so lucky. That's why it's incredibly important to make sure you watch your portions when dealing with making foods from your menu.

Portion control generally determines how much of every ingredient goes into each instance of that dish that's made for customers. So, if you were to get a seafood dish, the amount of certain seafood, like shrimp, will be significantly limited to allow the recipe more 'wiggle room' and save costs on getting ingredients for those particular dishes.

You can always learn how to use portion control through measuring out every ingredient that will go into your menu for your food truck. Measuring, well, everything can help you understand what and how you'll end up making certain recipes, particularly if it's already your first time managing your own food truck. So, you're not really alone in that regard.

Pre-measuring your food portions also helps you accomplish another important thing: it helps you save on both the costs to produce your food truck meals and it prevents you from wasting an excessive amount of money on food production. Portion control, alone, is pretty much important to think about when you're developing your food truck menu.

Let's Make a Well Balanced Food Truck Menu

So... You already have an idea in mind about the type of food truck menu you want, though you're not entirely sure about how to structure that menu. And, if you do know how to structure that menu, what's the best 'time' to serve certain foods?

To start, just know that food markets are known to be rather volatile. So, they're always changing between seasons. What sells like hotcakes in the winter (usually hot beverages) doesn't usually sell well in the summer... at least, not as well as ice-cold beverages.

Some of the 'externally occurring' factors that can influence your food market include the weather, the seasons and, yes, even the price of gas.

We also didn't mention another important factor—and that factor specifically involves the cost of buying these particular products in bulk. When we mean products, we mean the food, supplies, packaging and, sometimes, the active advertisement campaign belonging to your food truck.

Sometimes, the prices change so much that you need to actually only sell certain products when the prices change back to 'normal' again. That usually accounts for seasonal food and beverages, which are usually only available for a certain amount of time before, you guessed it, they're out of season.

You can probably include a handful of more expensive items, but do know that these items usually need more attention, in terms of their preparation.

If you do end up adding a few expensive items to your menu, you can always balance out those items with cheaper items that may take fewer resources to sell. Of course, it doesn't hurt to just include items on your food truck menu that are not only simple to prepare, but less expensive to prepare on a regular basis in your food truck.

Recipes, Food Truck Menus... And Preparing Them All

It's no secret that food trucks are fast becoming one of the more popular business opportunities in places where people know they can sell food. While it's not the easiest or least expensive business opportunity, it's an opportunity where people are at least guaranteed profits in the end... especially if they're smart about that.

One of the smartest things you could do for a food truck business is make up a menu that's bound to impress anyone that comes across that same food truck. While we actually reviewed the process of managing and creating that menu, it's about time we actually took a look at the actual food and beverages themselves.

Food Ideas For Food Trucks?

When you hear 'food trucks,' you're probably already thinking about several beverages and food items associated with the food trucks in your city. Some people may immediately associate that with kebabs and gyros, while others associate food trucks with just hot dogs. Given that any type of foods can be sold in food trucks, there's a wide variety of things that you actually do with food trucks.

So, what type of foods should you include in your food truck? Well, the easiest answer to that question is 'whatever you want.' Though, it's not that simple. You also have to learn more about what foods actually sell, what potential customers might like, how certain foods may sell in your area and many other factors that influence all of the associated costs.

Recipe Ideas For Food Truck Menus

With that in mind, you might find our suggestions for food truck ideas somewhat useful. The following food truck food ideas were inspired from a food truck resource, so these ideas are tried and tested and drawn from successful food truck outings across the country.

We're also going to include some paraphrased recipes from other resources, just to give you an idea about how simple recipes that relate to these food truck ideas can be. And, now, let's take a look at those recipes:

Barbeque

Barbeque, or simply BBQ, is one of the most low cost restaurant food options—especially when you take the cost to produce BBQ into consideration. While many BBQ dishes do require a lot of prep work, the overheads on these dishes aren't as high as you'd think... not to mention, that people pretty much love BBQ already.

BBQ can be a pretty portable food, too, particularly if you make BBQ on individual skewers. That turns a relatively messy (but good) dish into a great portable lunch with lasting appeal.

BBQ Turkey Legs

What they are: large, tender turkey legs prepared in a classic tomato-based barbeque sauce or teriyaki sauce. These can be pre-grilled before serving to buyers or even oven-baked and finished on a grill before keeping them warm on your truck. Good as a filling 'portable lunch' or a hearty snack.

Preparation and Cook Time: 45 minutes to 1 hour 30 minutes. Should be pre-prepared before serving via truck.

Ingredients:
- Turkey legs, cleaned and seasoned with your choice of spices or marinade

Barbeque sauce:
- 1 onion, finely chopped
- ½ cup of celery, finely chopped
- 2 tablespoons of both brown sugar and mustard
- 1 x 8 ounce can tomato sauce
- 1 cup water
- ½ cup ketchup
- 1 tablespoon of both butter and Worcestershire sauce

How to Cook:
Cook onions and celery in the butter until it gets soft. Add the other barbeque sauce ingredients and mix well. Remove from heat.

Cook turkey legs on a grill, with the fire set to medium hot. Cover the turkey legs to cook about 45 minutes to an hour before they're finished. Start basting them once they're just about done with your sauce.

Alternatively, you can cook these turkey legs in the over to cut costs.

Thai BBQ Grilled Chicken Recipe

What they are: This is another BBQ essential that can be alternatively pre-prepared in the oven to cut both time and costs. These tender pieces of chicken are prepared in a tangy, garlicky and sweet and sour sauce.

Preparation And Cook Time: About an hour to 1 hour and 30 minutes. Should be pre-prepared before serving on your food truck.

Ingredients:
- 1/2 fresh chicken, cut into small portions. You can also use chicken thighs, cut to size.

The marinade:
- 2 tablespoons of soy sauce, brown sugar and fish sauce
- 1 tablespoon each of black peppercorns (ground with coffee grinder) and dark soy sauce
- 3 tablespoons of sherry or cooking sherry. Can be omitted, if preferred.
- 10 minced garlic cloves

Dipping glaze:
- ½ cup of vinegar, such as white, white wine, rice or apple cider
- ⅓ cup brown sugar, slightly packed
- 1 tablespoons of soy sauce and fish sauce
- ⅓ to ½ dried, crushed chili flakes and/or cayenne pepper
- 4 minced garlic cloves

How to Cook:

Another dish best pre-prepared, start by combining all of the ingredients in the bowl by stirring to disperse the sugar. Add in the chicken and mix everything to ensure all of the chicken is well covered. Marinate this mixture overnight, if you can.

Make the dipping sauce and glaze by heating all of its ingredients together in a sauce pan. Bring it to a boil, allowing the glaze to simmer for a good 15 minutes. Cut the heat and let the sauce cool until serving time.
To cook the chicken, use a grill pan to prepare it well in advance. Place that chicken onto a grill pan or a pan lined with foil. Cook at 375 ° F for about 45 minutes, or until everything finishes cooking. Base the chicken with the glaze and then turn the oven's heat to finish off the chicken after glazing it.

Cupcakes And Other Sweet Treats

Although some people may be 'gourmet cupcaked' out after the trend hit the food world just few years back, cupcakes are just too eternally popular to go away. Gourmet cupcakes, especially if you design your menu around them, provide a creative take on an all dessert menu. I mean, you can't really go wrong with making a menu that features different cupcake flavors!

Though, you don't have to make a cupcake truck. You can have your menu feature any type of dessert you might want there in the first place. Some people end up using certain seasons, like the summer, to serve seasonal desserts like ice cream.

Vanilla and Chocolate Chip Cupcakes

What they are: sweet, decadent and, ultimately, simple to make for any food truck. Pre-make these sweet treats and wrap them in decorative wrappers and/or plastic wrap to keep them moist. These cupcakes are sweet enough on their own and don't actually need frosting... if you don't want frosting. In addition, this recipe can be used as a base for most cupcakes, including plain vanilla cupcakes.

Preparation and Cook Time: about 30 minutes, makes at least 24 to 36 cupcakes per batch.

❖ 1 cup of softened butter and milk

- ❖ 2 teaspoons of vanilla extract and baking powder
- ❖ 2 ½ cups of flour
- ❖ 1 ½ cups of sugar
- ❖ 4 large eggs
- ❖ A pinch of salt
- ❖ chocolate chips or chopped semi-sweet chocolate (optional, if you want)

How to Cook:

Use a mixer to beat together the butter and sugar until creamy and fluffy. Add each egg as you mix, ensuring that each egg gets thoroughly mixed into the butter-sugar mix. Add in vanilla as you mix.

Combine the dry ingredients (baking powder, salt and flour) with the creamed butter and sugar mix; add milk and beat the moisture until the batter becomes thick and smooth.

Use a muffin tin with paper liners to prepare these cupcakes, so they can be easily packed for sale aboard your food truck. Spoon the cupcake batter into each liner; you can sprinkle on the chocolate chips or pieces, if you want.

Bake the cupcakes in a preheated 375 ° F oven for about 15 to 17 minutes or until they're golden brown. If you insert in a toothpick, it should come out clean. These cupcakes can be stored, wrapped well, for several days at room temperature long after they're done cooling.

Different Types Of Sandwiches

Can you ever really go wrong with a sandwich? Not only that, the relatively 'linear' nature of preparing a sandwich makes them a great food to include on any food truck menu. Even though sandwiches can use many ingredients, you can easily balance costs by paying close attention to how you utilize those ingredients. It doesn't hurt that you can easily make back those costs—since, well, there's practically a popular sandwich for every region in the United States.

One of the most popular sandwiches that are an integral part of food truck menus is the Panini sandwich. Panini sandwiches are pretty easy to prepare and don't require any major equipment to prepare, besides a few Panini presses and other essential sandwich making supplies. Since Paninis make a great lunch, dinner and even breakfast food, you pretty much have a great set of options to potentially make the best Paninis on your block (go ahead and try that)!

Simple Chicken Panini

What this is: A tasty, classic Panini that can be cooked in a press-grill or a Panini press. It makes a great food truck recipe, thanks to its easy preparation and low ingredients list. All of the ingredients used in this dish are cooked, so you don't have to do any additional prep work.

Preparation and Cook Time: about 20 minutes for assembly and cooking several Panini.

Ingredients (for one Panini each):
- 2 slices of bread
- 1 or 2 slices of pre-cooked bacon
- Grilled chicken breasts and/or shredded rotisserie chicken, about 1 ½ cup for 1 sandwich
- 2 slices of provolone cheese
- 1 tablespoon of butter and prepared pesto

How to Cook:
Spread butter on one side of both bread slices. Turn over the slices and spread pesto on the other sides; top that side with your ingredients—bacon, chicken pieces and the cheese. Top with the other bread slice, placing the buttered side face up.

Cook on a preheated press-grill or Panini press until it's golden brown. Cut Panini to serve immediately.

Try Your Regional Cuisine

As mentioned, there's practically a 'sandwich for every major region of the United States,' so, there's naturally certain foods that are staples there, too. Whether you have chowder in the Northeast, BBQ in Texas, and an endless array of Southern comfort food within in the South, 'the best pizza' in several places throughout the North, there's always some type of regional food that regional natives just adore.

If you live in a part of the country where there's a regional favorite, why not put your own twist on a tried and true classic? You never know if it might take off—if it does, you'll pretty much have a steady bestseller in your hands!

Sweet Potato Steak Fries

What they are: These classic Southern comfort fries make great treats when on the go, so they pretty much make the perfect food truck menu item—particularly if the truck is already outfitted with the right equipment. You can use pretty much any variety of sweet potato or yam in this recipe. If you already have a menu with potato fries, you can use these fries as an alternative to regular potato fare.

Preparation and Cook Time: about 20 minutes, should be cooked fresh on the truck and kept warm.

Ingredients:
- Large sweet potatoes or yams, washed and dried
- Frying oil (canola, peanut or vegetable)
- Salt and pepper
- Your spice blends of choice (some people like it spicy, some people like it tangy, etc)

How to Cook:

Pre-wash your sweet potatoes and cut them into long, thin strips. The strips should be about a ¼ inch thick; soak them in ice water for at least 15 minutes. Have your deep fryer warming (to about 350 ° F) while you're preparing the fries—it's good to take care of this before the lunch rush! Take out the fries from the water and completely dry them.

Place the fries into the oil and fry for at least 5 minutes, until they're golden brown. Take them out when brown and let drain in fry basket. Place them into their warming compartment and season before serving to customers.

Classic Steak Fajitas

What they are: Another classic Mexican American street food, best known in its distinctly Southern American form. Prepare this dish overnight and finish on your food truck to serve the freshest dish possible. These recipes uses skirt steak, though you can use any inexpensive cut of steak in this recipe—and even substitute other meats and vegetables.

Preparation and Cook Time: about 40 minutes to prepare and cook, marinates overnight. Finish on food truck.

Ingredients:
- Beef flank steak, about 1 ½ pounds
- Medium-sized bell peppers, prepared and cut (red, yellow and green)
- Large onion, cut and prepared (Vidalia or other sweet onions)
- Scallions, cut and prepared (white and green)
- Ripened medium Haas avocados, cut and prepared
- Shredded lettuce
- Flour tortillas, wrapped in foil and stacked
- Bottled salsa—keep several varieties on hand!
- Sour cream, chopped cilantro, chopped chilies and other condiments

Prepared marinade, if you want to save time and costs. Usually uses a base of:
- Worcestershire sauce
- Vegetable oil (or another oil)
- Citrus juice (usually lime or lemon)

How to Cook:

Marinate the already prepared steak overnight; that also goes for any alternative meats and vegetables you may use to make these fajitas. Cook the steak aboard your food truck, ensuring that the skillet and/or grill you have are pre-oiled and on medium-high heat. Once cooked until it's at a customer's preferences, let the steak rest before cutting.

Add more oil to the pan and cook the vegetables, ensuing that they're well-seasoned and tender after about 6 or so minutes. You can warm the tortillas on another skillet or oven until they're ready for use.

Cut the steak after it rests for about 5 to 10 minutes, slicing the meat across the grain. After that, you can start the assembly, starting by taking a tortilla wrap and placing slices of meat in the center. Top with the customer's preferred cooked vegetables and condiments. Roll up the fajita to wrap it up and serve it to your customers.

Don't Forget About Local Organic Fare, Too

While you likely will be using much of your city's local food resources like, say, a farmer's market, there's nothing wrong with buying some of the healthier food options to creative organic alternatives for your own food truck menu.

After all, there's nothing wrong with having a few alternatives on hand. Having some vegetarian or even vegan options on your menu will help retain customers who may have not bought food from you in the past. Of course, you will have to have a separate cooking area for these particular foods, mainly to prevent contamination between the non-vegetarian or vegan foods that you already cook.

Getting your food 'sourced' directly from your home region can help potentially keep your business costs low, since you may have to order many ingredients in bulk at one time. For foods like meats and vegetables, buying locally can pretty much be a great money saving solution.

Cozy Vegetarian Chili

What this is: A tasty, vegetarian chili that can be enjoyed by a wide variety of eaters. While you can use canned ingredients, pre-prepared and frozen vegetables work best to ensure that it remains as fresh as possible... while remaining on a budget.

There's nothing wrong with also using fresh, local ingredients, too. Cook this in large batches overnight to let the flavors settle and reheat on the truck before serving to customers. After all, many types of chili are very 'reheat friendly' foods!

Preparation and Cook Time: about 1 hour, before serving the next day. 20 to 30 minutes to reheat.

Ingredients (use at your own preference):
Chili base makes one batch:
- 2 tablespoons of olive oil
- ¼ cup of vegetable broth
- 2 tablespoons of chili powder
- ½ teaspoon of both salt and pepper.
- ½ cup of textured vegetable protein and ½ cup of water.
- 1 can of diced tomatoes and tomato paste/plain tomato sauce (optional)

Chili ingredients:
- 1 can of black beans or pinto beans, drained and washed
- 1 can of kidney beans, drained and washed
- ½ onion, cut and prepared
- 3 cloves of garlic, cut and prepared (minced)
- 1 bell pepper, cut and prepared

- a dash of both cayenne pepper and red pepper flakes

How to Cook:
Sautee the onions, bell pepper and garlic together in the olive oil, in a large soup pot. After the ingredients become slightly brown, add in the tomatoes, chili powder and vegetable broth. Stir and let it simmer for a while before adding in the tomato sauce.

Reduce the heat to about medium low and add in the beans. Stir and cook for about 20 minutes. After about 20 minutes, add in the textured vegetable protein and water. You can actually cook this chili for longer than 20 minutes, keeping on low. Don't forget to add a bit of cayenne and red pepper flakes to add a spicy touch to your veggie chili.

This chili can be reheated aboard your truck, provided you have the equipment to handle serving large pots of soups and chilies. Of course, with many people, this dish will be a sure hit!

Are You Ready To Get Into The Mobile Food Business?

The mobile food business represents one of the hottest business opportunities out there. Though, even the most eager and successful mobile food business people have their doubts.

It's a conditional business. You do have to, well, be in the right place at the right time to hit it big. And, when you hit it big, you have to figure out how to maintain that momentum. That's not taking all of the costs and food management aspects of the business into consideration.

Even though getting there seems difficult, it's not that hard. Anyone, as long as they have the drive, can get started with their own food truck business in this day and age. It's a business that literally takes about a year or so to establish, but it's well worth the wait.

So, whether you're just securing funding or making up cool recipes, have fun getting into the mobile food industry. Since, it's certainly an industry that's here to stay.

Conclusion

Thank you again for downloading this book!

Finally, if you enjoyed this book, please take the time to share your thoughts and post a review on Amazon. It'd be greatly appreciated!

Thank you and good luck!

05104 7764

KNAPP BRANCH LIBRARY
13330 CONANT
DETROIT, MICHIGAN 48212
(313) 481-1772